MW00955958
Celebrating

Welcome
Baby

Dear ....

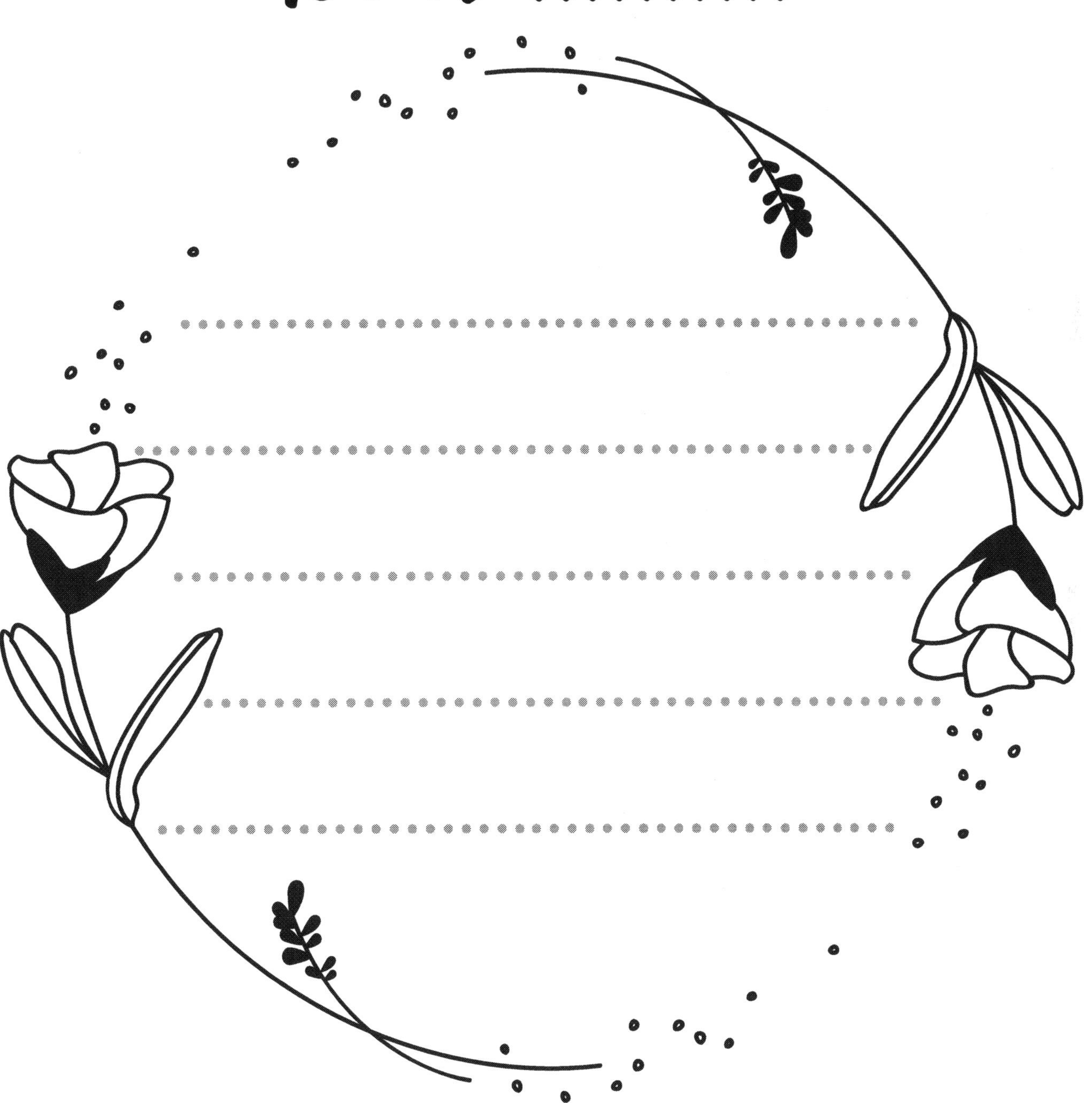

Name

Address

e-mail

predictions for the Baby

Gender

Date Of Birth

Time Of Birth

Eyes

Hair

Resemblance ○ Mom ○ Dad

I hope The Baby Gets

Dad's

I hope The Baby Gets

Mom's

Wishes for the Baby

Advice for parents

Guests

Name

Address

e-mail

predictions for the Baby

Gender

Date Of Birth

Time Of Birth

Eyes

Hair

Resemblance ○ Mom ○ Dad

I hope The Baby Gets
Dad's

I hope The Baby Gets
Mom's

Wishes for the Baby

Advice for parents

Guests

Name

Address

e-mail

predictions for the Baby

Gender

Date Of Birth

Time Of Birth

Eyes

Hair

Resemblance ○ Mom ○ Dad

I hope The Baby Gets Dad's

I hope The Baby Gets Mom's

Wishes for the Baby

Advice for parents

Guests

Name

Address

e-mail

predictions for the Baby

Gender

Date Of Birth

Time Of Birth

Eyes

Hair

Resemblance ○ Mom ○ Dad

I hope The Baby Gets Dad's

I hope The Baby Gets Mom's

Wishes for the Baby

Advice for parents

Guests

Name

Address

e-mail

predictions for the Baby

Gender

Date Of Birth

Time Of Birth

Eyes

Hair

Resemblance ○ Mom ○ Dad

I hope The Baby Gets

Dad's

I hope The Baby Gets

Mom's

Wishes for the Baby

Advice for parents

Guests

Name

Address

e-mail

predictions for the Baby

Gender

Date Of Birth

Time Of Birth

Eyes

Hair

Resemblance ○ Mom ○ Dad

I hope The Baby Gets

Dad's

I hope The Baby Gets

Mom's

Wishes for the Baby

Advice for parents

Name

Address

e-mail

predictions for the Baby

Gender

Date Of Birth

Time Of Birth

Eyes

Hair

Resemblance ○ Mom ○ Dad

I hope The Baby Gets

Dad's

I hope The Baby Gets

Mom's

Wishes for the Baby

Advice for parents

Guests

Name

Address

e-mail

predictions for the Baby

Gender

Date Of Birth

Time Of Birth

Eyes

Hair

Resemblance ○ Mom ○ Dad

I hope The Baby Gets

Dad's

I hope The Baby Gets

Mom's

Wishes for the Baby

Advice for parents

Guests

Name

Address

e-mail

predictions for the Baby

Gender

Date Of Birth

Time Of Birth

Eyes

Hair

Resemblance ○ Mom ○ Dad

I hope The Baby Gets

Dad's

I hope The Baby Gets

Mom's

Wishes for the Baby

Advice for parents

Name

Address

e-mail

predictions for the Baby

Gender

Date Of Birth

Time Of Birth

Eyes

Hair

Resemblance ○ Mom ○ Dad

I hope The Baby Gets Dad's

I hope The Baby Gets Mom's

Wishes for the Baby

Advice for parents

Guests

Name

Address

e-mail

predictions for the Baby

Gender

Date Of Birth

Time Of Birth

Eyes

Hair

Resemblance ○ Mom ○ Dad

I hope The Baby Gets

Dad's

I hope The Baby Gets

Mom's

Wishes for the Baby

Advice for parents

Guests

Name

Address

e-mail

predictions for the Baby

Gender

Date Of Birth

Time Of Birth

Eyes

Hair

Resemblance ○ Mom ○ Dad

I hope The Baby Gets
Dad's

I hope The Baby Gets
Mom's

Wishes for the Baby

Advice for parents

Guests

Name
Address
e-mail

predictions for the Baby

Gender
Date Of Birth
Time Of Birth
Eyes
Hair
Resemblance ○ Mom ○ Dad

I hope The Baby Gets
Dad's

I hope The Baby Gets
Mom's

Wishes for the Baby

Advice for parents

Guests

Name

Address

e-mail

predictions for the Baby

Gender

Date Of Birth

Time Of Birth

Eyes

Hair

Resemblance ○ Mom ○ Dad

I hope The Baby Gets Dad's

I hope The Baby Gets Mom's

Wishes for the Baby

Advice for parents

Guests

Name

Address

e-mail

predictions for the Baby

Gender

Date Of Birth

Time Of Birth

Eyes

Hair

Resemblance ○ Mom ○ Dad

I hope The Baby Gets

Dad's

I hope The Baby Gets

Mom's

Wishes for the Baby

Advice for parents

Name

Address

e-mail

predictions for the Baby

Gender

Date Of Birth

Time Of Birth

Eyes

Hair

Resemblance ○ Mom ○ Dad

I hope The Baby Gets

Dad's

I hope The Baby Gets

Mom's

Wishes for the Baby

Advice for parents

Guests

Name

Address

e-mail

predictions for the Baby

Gender

Date Of Birth

Time Of Birth

Eyes

Hair

Resemblance ○ Mom ○ Dad

I hope The Baby Gets

Dad's

I hope The Baby Gets

Mom's

Wishes for the Baby

Advice for parents

Guests

Name

Address

e-mail

predictions for the Baby

Gender

Date Of Birth

Time Of Birth

Eyes

Hair

Resemblance ○ Mom ○ Dad

I hope The Baby Gets Dad's

I hope The Baby Gets Mom's

Wishes for the Baby

Advice for parents

Guests

Name

Address

e-mail

predictions for the Baby

Gender

Date Of Birth

Time Of Birth

Eyes

Hair

Resemblance ○ Mom ○ Dad

I hope The Baby Gets

Dad's

I hope The Baby Gets

Mom's

Wishes for the Baby

Advice for parents

Guests

Name

Address

e-mail

predictions for the Baby

Gender

Date Of Birth

Time Of Birth

Eyes

Hair

Resemblance ○ Mom ○ Dad

I hope The Baby Gets

Dad's

I hope The Baby Gets

Mom's

Wishes for the Baby

Advice for parents

Guests

Name

Address

e-mail

predictions for the Baby

Gender

Date Of Birth

Time Of Birth

Eyes

Hair

Resemblance ○ Mom ○ Dad

I hope The Baby Gets Dad's

I hope The Baby Gets Mom's

Wishes for the Baby

Advice for parents

Guests

Name

Address

e-mail

predictions for the Baby

Gender

Date Of Birth

Time Of Birth

Eyes

Hair

Resemblance ○ Mom ○ Dad

I hope The Baby Gets Dad's

I hope The Baby Gets Mom's

Wishes for the Baby

Advice for parents

Guests

Name

Address

e-mail

predictions for the Baby

Gender

Date Of Birth

Time Of Birth

Eyes

Hair

Resemblance ○ Mom ○ Dad

I hope The Baby Gets
Dad's

I hope The Baby Gets
Mom's

Wishes for the Baby

Advice for parents

Guests

Name

Address

e-mail

predictions for the Baby

Gender

Date Of Birth

Time Of Birth

Eyes

Hair

Resemblance ○ Mom ○ Dad

I hope The Baby Gets Dad's

I hope The Baby Gets Mom's

Wishes for the Baby

Advice for parents

Guests

Name

Address

e-mail

predictions for the Baby

Gender

Date Of Birth

Time Of Birth

Eyes

Hair

Resemblance ○ Mom ○ Dad

I hope The Baby Gets Dad's

I hope The Baby Gets Mom's

Wishes for the Baby

Advice for parents

Guests

Name

Address

e-mail

predictions for the Baby

Gender

Date Of Birth

Time Of Birth

Eyes

Hair

Resemblance Mom Dad

I hope The Baby Gets Dad's

I hope The Baby Gets Mom's

Wishes for the Baby

Advice for parents

Guests

Name

Address

e-mail

predictions for the Baby

Gender

Date Of Birth

Time Of Birth

Eyes

Hair

Resemblance ○ Mom ○ Dad

I hope The Baby Gets

Dad's

I hope The Baby Gets

Mom's

Wishes for the Baby

Advice for parents

Name

Address

e-mail

predictions for the Baby

Gender

Date Of Birth

Time Of Birth

Eyes

Hair

Resemblance ○ Mom ○ Dad

I hope The Baby Gets Dad's

I hope The Baby Gets Mom's

Wishes for the Baby

Advice for parents

Name

Address

e-mail

predictions for the Baby

Gender

Date Of Birth

Time Of Birth

Eyes

Hair

Resemblance ○ Mom ○ Dad

I hope The Baby Gets
Dad's

I hope The Baby Gets
Mom's

Wishes for the Baby

Advice for parents

Guests

Name

Address

e-mail

predictions for the Baby

Gender

Date Of Birth

Time Of Birth

Eyes

Hair

Resemblance ○ Mom ○ Dad

I hope The Baby Gets

Dad's

I hope The Baby Gets

Mom's

Wishes for the Baby

Advice for parents

Guests

Name

Address

e-mail

predictions for the Baby

Gender

Date Of Birth

Time Of Birth

Eyes

Hair

Resemblance ○ Mom ○ Dad

I hope The Baby Gets

Dad's

I hope The Baby Gets

Mom's

Wishes for the Baby

Advice for parents

Guests

Name

Address

e-mail

predictions for the Baby

Gender

Date Of Birth

Time Of Birth

Eyes

Hair

Resemblance ○ Mom ○ Dad

I hope The Baby Gets Dad's

I hope The Baby Gets Mom's

Wishes for the Baby

Advice for parents

Guests

Name

Address

e-mail

predictions for the Baby

Gender

Date Of Birth

Time Of Birth

Eyes

Hair

Resemblance ○ Mom ○ Dad

I hope The Baby Gets Dad's

I hope The Baby Gets Mom's

Wishes for the Baby

Advice for parents

Guests

Name
Address
e-mail

predictions for the Baby

Gender
Date Of Birth
Time Of Birth
Eyes
Hair
Resemblance ◯ Mom ◯ Dad

I hope The Baby Gets
Dad's

I hope The Baby Gets
Mom's

Wishes for the Baby

Advice for parents

Guests

Name

Address

e-mail

predictions for the Baby

Gender

Date Of Birth

Time Of Birth

Eyes

Hair

Resemblance ○ Mom ○ Dad

I hope The Baby Gets Dad's

I hope The Baby Gets Mom's

Wishes for the Baby

Advice for parents

Guests

Name

Address

e-mail

predictions for the Baby

Gender

Date Of Birth

Time Of Birth

Eyes

Hair

Resemblance ○ Mom ○ Dad

I hope The Baby Gets

Dad's

I hope The Baby Gets

Mom's

Wishes for the Baby

Advice for parents

Guests

Name

Address

e-mail

predictions for the Baby

Gender

Date Of Birth

Time Of Birth

Eyes

Hair

Resemblance ○ Mom ○ Dad

I hope The Baby Gets

Dad's

I hope The Baby Gets

Mom's

Wishes for the Baby

Advice for parents

Name

Address

e-mail

predictions for the Baby

Gender

Date Of Birth

Time Of Birth

Eyes

Hair

Resemblance ○ Mom ○ Dad

I hope The Baby Gets Dad's

I hope The Baby Gets Mom's

Wishes for the Baby

Advice for parents

Name

Address

e-mail

predictions for the Baby

Gender

Date Of Birth

Time Of Birth

Eyes

Hair

Resemblance ○ Mom ○ Dad

I hope The Baby Gets Dad's

I hope The Baby Gets Mom's

Wishes for the Baby

Advice for parents

Guests

Name

Address

e-mail

predictions for the Baby

Gender

Date Of Birth

Time Of Birth

Eyes

Hair

Resemblance ○ Mom ○ Dad

I hope The Baby Gets Dad's

I hope The Baby Gets Mom's

Wishes for the Baby

Advice for parents

Guests

Name

Address

e-mail

predictions for the Baby

Gender

Date Of Birth

Time Of Birth

Eyes

Hair

Resemblance ○ Mom ○ Dad

I hope The Baby Gets Dad's

I hope The Baby Gets Mom's

Wishes for the Baby

Advice for parents

Guests

Name

Address

e-mail

predictions for the Baby

Gender

Date Of Birth

Time Of Birth

Eyes

Hair

Resemblance ○ Mom ○ Dad

I hope The Baby Gets Dad's

I hope The Baby Gets Mom's

Wishes for the Baby

Advice for parents

Guests

Name

Address

e-mail

predictions for the Baby

Gender

Date Of Birth

Time Of Birth

Eyes

Hair

Resemblance ○ Mom ○ Dad

I hope The Baby Gets

Dad's

I hope The Baby Gets

Mom's

Wishes for the Baby

Advice for parents

Guests

Name

Address

e-mail

predictions for the Baby

Gender

Date Of Birth

Time Of Birth

Eyes

Hair

Resemblance ○ Mom ○ Dad

I hope The Baby Gets Dad's

I hope The Baby Gets Mom's

Wishes for the Baby

Advice for parents

Name

Address

e-mail

predictions for the Baby

Gender

Date Of Birth

Time Of Birth

Eyes

Hair

Resemblance ○ Mom ○ Dad

I hope The Baby Gets Dad's

I hope The Baby Gets Mom's

Wishes for the Baby

Advice for parents

Guests

Name

Address

e-mail

predictions for the Baby

Gender

Date Of Birth

Time Of Birth

Eyes

Hair

Resemblance ○ Mom ○ Dad

I hope The Baby Gets

Dad's

I hope The Baby Gets

Mom's

Wishes for the Baby

Advice for parents

Guests

Name

Address

e-mail

predictions for the Baby

Gender

Date Of Birth

Time Of Birth

Eyes

Hair

Resemblance ○ Mom ○ Dad

I hope The Baby Gets

Dad's

I hope The Baby Gets

Mom's

Wishes for the Baby

Advice for parents

Name

Address

e-mail

predictions for the Baby

Gender

Date Of Birth

Time Of Birth

Eyes

Hair

Resemblance ○ Mom ○ Dad

I hope The Baby Gets
Dad's

I hope The Baby Gets
Mom's

Wishes for the Baby

Advice for parents

Guests

Name

Address

e-mail

predictions for the Baby

Gender

Date Of Birth

Time Of Birth

Eyes

Hair

Resemblance ○ Mom ○ Dad

I hope The Baby Gets

Dad's

I hope The Baby Gets

Mom's

Wishes for the Baby

Advice for parents

Guests

Name

Address

e-mail

predictions for the Baby

Gender

Date Of Birth

Time Of Birth

Eyes

Hair

Resemblance ○ Mom ○ Dad

I hope The Baby Gets

Dad's

I hope The Baby Gets

Mom's

Wishes for the Baby

Advice for parents

Guests

Name

Address

e-mail

predictions for the Baby

Gender

Date Of Birth

Time Of Birth

Eyes

Hair

Resemblance ○ Mom ○ Dad

I hope The Baby Gets

Dad's

I hope The Baby Gets

Mom's

Wishes for the Baby

Advice for parents

Guests

Name

Address

e-mail

predictions for the Baby

Gender

Date Of Birth

Time Of Birth

Eyes

Hair

Resemblance ○ Mom ○ Dad

I hope The Baby Gets

Dad's

I hope The Baby Gets

Mom's

Wishes for the Baby

Advice for parents

Guests

Name

Address

e-mail

predictions for the Baby

Gender

Date Of Birth

Time Of Birth

Eyes

Hair

Resemblance ○ Mom ○ Dad

I hope The Baby Gets Dad's

I hope The Baby Gets Mom's

Wishes for the Baby

Advice for parents

Guests

Name

Address

e-mail

predictions for the Baby

Gender

Date Of Birth

Time Of Birth

Eyes

Hair

Resemblance ○ Mom ○ Dad

I hope The Baby Gets Dad's

I hope The Baby Gets Mom's

Wishes for the Baby

Advice for parents

Name

Address

e-mail

predictions for the Baby

Gender

Date Of Birth

Time Of Birth

Eyes

Hair

Resemblance ○ Mom ○ Dad

I hope The Baby Gets Dad's

I hope The Baby Gets Mom's

Wishes for the Baby

Advice for parents

Guests

Name

Address

e-mail

predictions for the Baby

Gender

Date Of Birth

Time Of Birth

Eyes

Hair

Resemblance ○ Mom ○ Dad

I hope The Baby Gets

Dad's

I hope The Baby Gets

Mom's

Wishes for the Baby

Advice for parents

Name

Address

e-mail

predictions for the Baby

Gender

Date Of Birth

Time Of Birth

Eyes

Hair

Resemblance ○ Mom ○ Dad

I hope The Baby Gets

Dad's

I hope The Baby Gets

Mom's

Wishes for the Baby

Advice for parents

Guests

Name

Address

e-mail

predictions for the Baby

Gender

Date Of Birth

Time Of Birth

Eyes

Hair

Resemblance ○ Mom ○ Dad

I hope The Baby Gets

Dad's

I hope The Baby Gets

Mom's

Wishes for the Baby

Advice for parents

Guests

Name

Address

e-mail

predictions for the Baby

Gender

Date Of Birth

Time Of Birth

Eyes

Hair

Resemblance ○ Mom ○ Dad

I hope The Baby Gets

Dad's

I hope The Baby Gets

Mom's

Wishes for the Baby

Advice for parents

Guests

Name
Address
e-mail

predictions for the Baby

Gender
Date Of Birth
Time Of Birth
Eyes
Hair
Resemblance ○ Mom ○ Dad

I hope The Baby Gets
Dad's

I hope The Baby Gets
Mom's

Wishes for the Baby

Advice for parents

Guests

Name

Address

e-mail

predictions for the Baby

Gender

Date Of Birth

Time Of Birth

Eyes

Hair

Resemblance ○ Mom ○ Dad

I hope The Baby Gets

Dad's

I hope The Baby Gets

Mom's

Wishes for the Baby

Advice for parents

Guests

Name

Address

e-mail

predictions for the Baby

Gender

Date Of Birth

Time Of Birth

Eyes

Hair

Resemblance ◯ Mom ◯ Dad

I hope The Baby Gets Dad's

I hope The Baby Gets Mom's

Wishes for the Baby

Advice for parents

Guests

Name

Address

e-mail

predictions for the Baby

Gender

Date Of Birth

Time Of Birth

Eyes

Hair

Resemblance ○ Mom ○ Dad

I hope The Baby Gets

Dad's

I hope The Baby Gets

Mom's

Wishes for the Baby

Advice for parents

Guests

Name

Address

e-mail

predictions for the Baby

Gender

Date Of Birth

Time Of Birth

Eyes

Hair

Resemblance ○ Mom ○ Dad

I hope The Baby Gets Dad's

I hope The Baby Gets Mom's

Wishes for the Baby

Advice for parents

Guests

Name

Address

e-mail

predictions for the Baby

Gender

Date Of Birth

Time Of Birth

Eyes

Hair

Resemblance ○ Mom ○ Dad

I hope The Baby Gets Dad's

I hope The Baby Gets Mom's

Wishes for the Baby

Advice for parents

Guests

Name

Address

e-mail

predictions for the Baby

Gender

Date Of Birth

Time Of Birth

Eyes

Hair

Resemblance ○ Mom ○ Dad

I hope The Baby Gets Dad's

I hope The Baby Gets Mom's

Wishes for the Baby

Advice for parents

Guests

Name

Address

e-mail

predictions for the Baby

Gender

Date Of Birth

Time Of Birth

Eyes

Hair

Resemblance ○ Mom ○ Dad

I hope The Baby Gets Dad's

I hope The Baby Gets Mom's

Wishes for the Baby

Advice for parents

Guests

Name

Address

e-mail

predictions for the Baby

Gender

Date Of Birth

Time Of Birth

Eyes

Hair

Resemblance ○ Mom ○ Dad

I hope The Baby Gets

Dad's

I hope The Baby Gets

Mom's

Wishes for the Baby

Advice for parents

Guests

Name

Address

e-mail

predictions for the Baby

Gender

Date Of Birth

Time Of Birth

Eyes

Hair

Resemblance ○ Mom ○ Dad

I hope The Baby Gets Dad's

I hope The Baby Gets Mom's

Wishes for the Baby

Advice for parents

Guests

Name

Address

e-mail

predictions for the Baby

Gender

Date Of Birth

Time Of Birth

Eyes

Hair

Resemblance ○ Mom ○ Dad

I hope The Baby Gets Dad's

I hope The Baby Gets Mom's

Wishes for the Baby

Advice for parents

Guests

Name

Address

e-mail

predictions for the Baby

Gender

Date Of Birth

Time Of Birth

Eyes

Hair

Resemblance ○ Mom ○ Dad

I hope The Baby Gets

Dad's

I hope The Baby Gets

Mom's

Wishes for the Baby

Advice for parents

Guests

Name

Address

e-mail

predictions for the Baby

Gender

Date Of Birth

Time Of Birth

Eyes

Hair

Resemblance Mom Dad

I hope The Baby Gets

Dad's

I hope The Baby Gets

Mom's

Wishes for the Baby

Advice for parents

Guests

Name

Address

e-mail

predictions for the Baby

Gender

Date Of Birth

Time Of Birth

Eyes

Hair

Resemblance ○ Mom ○ Dad

I hope The Baby Gets

Dad's

I hope The Baby Gets

Mom's

Wishes for the Baby

Advice for parents

Guests

Name

Address

e-mail

predictions for the Baby

Gender

Date Of Birth

Time Of Birth

Eyes

Hair

Resemblance ○ Mom ○ Dad

I hope The Baby Gets
Dad's

I hope The Baby Gets
Mom's

Wishes for the Baby

Advice for parents

Guests

Name

Address

e-mail

predictions for the Baby

Gender

Date Of Birth

Time Of Birth

Eyes

Hair

Resemblance ○ Mom ○ Dad

I hope The Baby Gets

Dad's

I hope The Baby Gets

Mom's

Wishes for the Baby

Advice for parents

Guests

Name

Address

e-mail

predictions for the Baby

Gender

Date Of Birth

Time Of Birth

Eyes

Hair

Resemblance ○ Mom ○ Dad

I hope The Baby Gets Dad's

I hope The Baby Gets Mom's

Wishes for the Baby

Advice for parents

Guests

Name

Address

e-mail

predictions for the Baby

Gender

Date Of Birth

Time Of Birth

Eyes

Hair

Resemblance ○ Mom ○ Dad

I hope The Baby Gets

Dad's

I hope The Baby Gets

Mom's

Wishes for the Baby

Advice for parents

Guests

Name

Address

e-mail

predictions for the Baby

Gender

Date Of Birth

Time Of Birth

Eyes

Hair

Resemblance ○ Mom ○ Dad

I hope The Baby Gets Dad's

I hope The Baby Gets Mom's

Wishes for the Baby

Advice for parents

Guests

Name

Address

e-mail

predictions for the Baby

Gender

Date Of Birth

Time Of Birth

Eyes

Hair

Resemblance ○ Mom ○ Dad

I hope The Baby Gets

Dad's

I hope The Baby Gets

Mom's

Wishes for the Baby

Advice for parents

Guests

Name

Address

e-mail

predictions for the Baby

Gender

Date Of Birth

Time Of Birth

Eyes

Hair

Resemblance ○ Mom ○ Dad

I hope The Baby Gets

Dad's

I hope The Baby Gets

Mom's

Wishes for the Baby

Advice for parents

Guests

Name

Address

e-mail

predictions for the Baby

Gender

Date Of Birth

Time Of Birth

Eyes

Hair

Resemblance ○ Mom ○ Dad

I hope The Baby Gets

Dad's

I hope The Baby Gets

Mom's

Wishes for the Baby

Advice for parents

Guests

Name

Address

e-mail

predictions for the Baby

Gender

Date Of Birth

Time Of Birth

Eyes

Hair

Resemblance ○ Mom ○ Dad

I hope The Baby Gets

Dad's

I hope The Baby Gets

Mom's

Wishes for the Baby

Advice for parents

Guests

Name

Address

e-mail

predictions for the Baby

Gender

Date Of Birth

Time Of Birth

Eyes

Hair

Resemblance ○ Mom ○ Dad

I hope The Baby Gets

Dad's

I hope The Baby Gets

Mom's

Wishes for the Baby

Advice for parents

Guests

Name

Address

e-mail

predictions for the Baby

Gender

Date Of Birth

Time Of Birth

Eyes

Hair

Resemblance ○ Mom ○ Dad

I hope The Baby Gets Dad's

I hope The Baby Gets Mom's

Wishes for the Baby

Advice for parents

Guests

Name

Address

e-mail

predictions for the Baby

Gender

Date Of Birth

Time Of Birth

Eyes

Hair

Resemblance ○ Mom ○ Dad

I hope The Baby Gets Dad's

I hope The Baby Gets Mom's

Wishes for the Baby

Advice for parents

Guests

Name

Address

e-mail

predictions for the Baby

Gender

Date Of Birth

Time Of Birth

Eyes

Hair

Resemblance ○ Mom ○ Dad

I hope The Baby Gets Dad's

I hope The Baby Gets Mom's

Wishes for the Baby

Advice for parents

Guests

Name

Address

e-mail

predictions for the Baby

Gender

Date Of Birth

Time Of Birth

Eyes

Hair

Resemblance ○ Mom ○ Dad

I hope The Baby Gets Dad's

I hope The Baby Gets Mom's

Wishes for the Baby

Advice for parents

Guests

Name

Address

e-mail

predictions for the Baby

Gender

Date Of Birth

Time Of Birth

Eyes

Hair

Resemblance ○ Mom ○ Dad

I hope The Baby Gets

Dad's

I hope The Baby Gets

Mom's

Wishes for the Baby

Advice for parents

Guests

Name

Address

e-mail

predictions for the Baby

Gender

Date Of Birth

Time Of Birth

Eyes

Hair

Resemblance ○ Mom ○ Dad

I hope The Baby Gets

Dad's

I hope The Baby Gets

Mom's

Wishes for the Baby

Advice for parents

Guests

Name

Address

e-mail

predictions for the Baby

Gender

Date Of Birth

Time Of Birth

Eyes

Hair

Resemblance ○ Mom ○ Dad

I hope The Baby Gets Dad's

I hope The Baby Gets Mom's

Wishes for the Baby

Advice for parents

Guests

Name

Address

e-mail

predictions for the Baby

Gender

Date Of Birth

Time Of Birth

Eyes

Hair

Resemblance ○ Mom ○ Dad

I hope The Baby Gets Dad's

I hope The Baby Gets Mom's

Wishes for the Baby

Advice for parents

Name

Address

e-mail

predictions for the Baby

Gender

Date Of Birth

Time Of Birth

Eyes

Hair

Resemblance ○ Mom ○ Dad

I hope The Baby Gets

Dad's

I hope The Baby Gets

Mom's

Wishes for the Baby

Advice for parents

Guests

Name

Address

e-mail

predictions for the Baby

Gender

Date Of Birth

Time Of Birth

Eyes

Hair

Resemblance ○ Mom ○ Dad

I hope The Baby Gets Dad's

I hope The Baby Gets Mom's

Wishes for the Baby

Advice for parents

Guests

Name

Address

e-mail

predictions for the Baby

Gender

Date Of Birth

Time Of Birth

Eyes

Hair

Resemblance ○ Mom ○ Dad

I hope The Baby Gets

Dad's

I hope The Baby Gets

Mom's

Wishes for the Baby

Advice for parents

Name

Address

e-mail

predictions for the Baby

Gender

Date Of Birth

Time Of Birth

Eyes

Hair

Resemblance ○ Mom ○ Dad

I hope The Baby Gets

Dad's

I hope The Baby Gets

Mom's

Wishes for the Baby

Advice for parents

Guests

Name

Address

e-mail

predictions for the Baby

Gender

Date Of Birth

Time Of Birth

Eyes

Hair

Resemblance ○ Mom ○ Dad

I hope The Baby Gets

Dad's

I hope The Baby Gets

Mom's

Wishes for the Baby

Advice for parents

Guests

Name

Address

e-mail

predictions for the Baby

Gender

Date Of Birth

Time Of Birth

Eyes

Hair

Resemblance ○ Mom ○ Dad

I hope The Baby Gets

Dad's

I hope The Baby Gets

Mom's

Wishes for the Baby

Advice for parents

Guests

Name

Address

e-mail

predictions for the Baby

Gender

Date Of Birth

Time Of Birth

Eyes

Hair

Resemblance ○ Mom ○ Dad

I hope The Baby Gets
Dad's

I hope The Baby Gets
Mom's

Wishes for the Baby

Advice for parents

Gift Log

Gift Received	Given By	Thank You Card

Gift Log

Gift Received	Given By	Thank You Card

Gift Log

Gift Received	Given By	Thank You Card

Gift Log

Gift Received	Given By	Thank You Card

Gift Log

Gift Received	Given By	Thank You Card

Gift Log

Gift Received	Given By	Thank You Card

Gift Log

Gift Received	Given By	Thank You Card

Gift Log

Gift Received	Given By	Thank You Card

Gift Log

Gift Received	Given By	Thank You Card

Gift Log

Gift Received	Given By	Thank You Card

Made in the USA
Monee, IL
15 November 2024